How to Make Boxes of Cash

With Self-Storage Auctions

by
Barbara Rogers

Bloomington, IN Milton Keynes, UK

AuthorHouse™
1663 Liberty Drive, Suite 200
Bloomington, IN 47403
www.authorhouse.com
Phone: 1-800-839-8640

© 2007 Barbara Rogers. All rights reserved.

No part of this book may be reproduced, stored in a retrieval system, or transmitted by any means without the written permission of the author.

First published by AuthorHouse 5/16/2007

ISBN: 978-1-4259-7860-0 (sc)

Printed in the United States of America
Bloomington, Indiana

This book is printed on acid-free paper.

I dedicate this book to my husband Jason, who always loves and understands me. Also,
my kids Chris and Jessica,
who are my reason and not my excuse!

Table of Contents

INTRODUCTION ix

CHAPTER 1
Is This the Right Business for You?
And the Benefits 1

CHAPTER 2
Tips on Attending Auctions, Bidding,
and Some Other Helpful Hints… 7

CHAPTER 3
"CRAP! I Won – NOW What????" 17

CHAPTER 4
What a Typical Week Should Look Like 25

CHAPTER 5
Some Valuable Tips 29

Epilogue 33

Introduction

A few years ago, I moved with my husband and about 100 of his closest friends (a unit in the army) to Arizona for a year. When his duty was up, we came home and I had to decide what business I wanted to get into.

We talked about a few ideas, and one came to mind. Not too many people know how to get into this business, but the work it provides is extremely flexible and you can make some serious money.

Maybe you are one of those people who gets that sick feeling in the pit of your stomach every Sunday night, because you know you will have to get up, get out of your nice, warm bed on Monday morning and go to a job that barely pays the bills and gives you absolutely NO satisfaction whatsoever. Or maybe you like your job but need some extra cash on the side to pay off some bills. Either way, I have discovered a great and well-hidden secret, which I will share with you in this book.

The secret I am talking about is **self-storage auctions**. Storage facilities hold auctions monthly, to clear out the tenants who have not paid their rent in several months. There is definitely no shortage of storage facilities…everywhere you look, there is one. Just in the San Francisco Bay area alone, there are more than 2,000 auctions held monthly.

With this choice of business, you are in charge of your own time and in charge of your future! Imagine that!

The reason this secret is well-hidden is because most of the attendees would rather the general public not know about these auctions at all, much less how to make a business out of attending them.

Think about it: Fewer people means less competition, which in turn means the locker contents are auctioned off cheaper, with higher profits for the auction attendees! However, if you read this book, take my advice, use the information in this book, and work smart (and sometimes hard!), you just might find those higher profits in your own pocket!

If you are willing to get out of your daily routine and try some simple ideas that ANYONE can do, you can make some money—and who knows—maybe you can find a treasure or two for yourself along the way!

I designed this book to be light reading, and something you can carry in your pocket so you can refer back to it whenever needed. I hope you enjoy reading this book, and find it full of valuable information.

At the end of the book, I have listed a URL to a Web site that I invite you to visit. It is there for you to share your thoughts, ideas, and storage-auction stories, and please feel free to e-mail me pictures of all the treasures you find!

Chapter 1

Is This the Right Business for You? And the Benefits

Business owners are a breed all their own, so you need to do some research to find out if you have the fortitude to be one. When deciding if this business is right for you, here are a few questions to get you thinking:

Do you love to find buried treasure?

If you get a thrill from opening up boxes that you haven't packed because of what you might find, this is the business for you.

Do you want a business that is flexible?

The flexible schedule is such a bonus, especially if you have kids! For instance: If your kids have a doctor appointment during the day, you can arrange your schedule around it. You are able to go to the auctions you want to attend, and fit your errands and other responsibilities in there as well. Many times, you will attend three or four auctions one day and zero the next, which gives you even more flexibility!

Are you willing to get out of a business what you put in?

This question really is about anything you do in life. **Few jobs will pay you to show up only when you feel like it**. So it makes sense that if you attend as many auctions as you can and are patient enough to wait for the great lockers, you will make more money!

BENEFITS

There are so many benefits not only to the storage-auctioning business, but to owning a business as well. I have listed below some of the benefits that appealed to me as I was doing my research.

Inexpensive way to furnish a home

Have you recently shopped for furniture? If not, try it. I recommend driving down to your local furniture store to see what a dining room set costs, or maybe a bedroom set. Talk about sticker shock!

Using storage auctions, my husband and I were able to move my mother into a three-bedroom home, spending less than $500 to furnish the entire place. If you keep an eye out for the lockers with furniture in them, you will eventually find one and pick it up for a song.

Usable and sellable household items

You can often find full sets of dishes, linens, decorative items, and other extremely useful things for yourself. However, other people shop for these household items all the time, so you will be able to resell them quickly at a sale.

If you already have an eBay store, secondhand store, or if you resell collectibles… this is an outstanding opportunity to find new inventory at a great price.

I am always running across items such as Danbury Mint and Franklin Mint collectibles, baseball cards, sports memorabilia, comics, records, and so much more. A great locker can more than pay for itself, sometimes with just one collectible item!

Also, you can get CDs and DVDs at minimal cost as well. The list of what you can find in the lockers goes on and on, but you get the idea!

An antiquing outlet

If you are in search of antiques or know someone who is, this is the way to go. You can find lockers full of treasures at rock-bottom prices!

One locker I purchased for $265 was a huge locker measuring fifteen feet by thirty feet. It was FULL of antiques. I found everything from glass negatives to antique tables!

Another example: One auction attendee who paid just over $200 for an entire locker found a Dirk Van Erp lamp made out of leather. Once word had spread about this great find, a rep from PBS's *Antiques Roadshow* made a house call, and valued the lamp at $150,000! Now, that is quite a return!

A great workout!

If you decide to unload the lockers yourself, you will definitely be sweating by the end of the day! What a great excuse to skip the gym!

Hidden treasures for the treasure hunter in all of us!

If you enjoy opening boxes that you did not pack because of the element of surprise, this is a definite treasure hunter's paradise. You might find hidden treasures like jewelry or even cash. I once found $200 cash in an envelope! I have also heard of one locker discovery: large dollar bills hidden in old books stored in grocery bags!

I once found three pamphlets in a locker created by Dr. Seuss. They were about putting advertising signs in La Jolla. I auctioned off two of them on eBay for $250 each! You can read the whole story on our Web site!

BEST OF ALL, you get the benefits of owning your own business…

You will have to research the tax benefits involved with owning a business, but they are there. I cannot think of a better way to get into business for yourself with minimal risk and minimal money up front.

Chapter 2

Tips on Attending Auctions, Bidding, and Some Other Helpful Hints…

Attending Auctions

You are going to want to get on an auctioneers' mailing list for upcoming auctions in your area. The best way to start from scratch is to call your local storage facilities and ask them when their auction/lien sales are. You might initially get a few clueless employees who have never heard of an auction, but keep calling…you will find some knowledgeable employees.

Once you have a list of upcoming auctions, this is what you need to do:

Prepare for your auction! This is critical to the success and outcome of the auctions you attend. Here are the steps:

1. Mark dates and times in a calendar.

2. Call and confirm auctions the day before.

    It is a bonus if you can get the manager to tell you the size, contents, or even the name of the owner of the locker(s). Once in awhile an owner of a locker will have multiple units come up for auction, so you might get an idea of the type of things that are in the lockers.

3. Go by the bank and get some cash. Some auctioneers will let you use credit cards; it does not hurt to ask. Also, be aware of any cleaning deposits or buyer's premium that the auctioneer may attach to the final bid.

    If you do bring cash, it is a good idea to bring at least $500, but more money is always a good idea.

4. Bring a padlock.

    It is very handy to have multiple locks keyed to one key.

5. Bring a flashlight.

Day of the auction:

This is the exciting part: attending the auction! You will want to arrive ten to fifteen minutes early.

BEFORE you bid on a locker, find out how long the manager of the storage facility will give you to clean the locker out; sometimes it is negotiable. The bigger the unit, the more time they will usually give you.

When the door rolls up, HERE IS WHAT TO LOOK FOR:

You want to spot....

Boxes that are unopened, taped, and labeled

Dust and mothball smell in a locker (possible antique locker)

A tenant who has been there for years (accumulates things in the locker and may have forgotten about stuff)

Try to see if you can spot...

What is IN some of the boxes

Legs of furniture

Any antique-looking furniture

The backs of furniture

The amount of trash...you would be amazed at how much trash people pay to store

The more experience you get, the more you will be able to spot these and other things quickly. I must warn you...you will have to do this while you are trying to make your way through the crowd. Other attendees will be looking for some of these things, too; the thing to remember is many important clues get overlooked by others. For instance, if nobody else saw an antique in the corner that YOU saw, you might be able to get the locker for five dollars!

Many times, you are not allowed to go in the locker or open any contents, so you will have to be able to spot stuff. Trust me, you will get good at it over time.

Here's where the fun begins. After you have looked at the contents in the locker, get a rough estimate in your head about how much you would be able to make from what you have seen. Now, in theory, you should only bid on what you see, but chances are you will not win the locker that way. You might have to take a risk and bid a little higher if it has many things you are looking for.

Bidding Advice

Note: My bidding experience has been in California, so the particulars might be different in other states. The auctioneers I have interviewed who work out of state say most of the auction laws are very similar across the country, but you will still want to check your local area's auction laws for any differences.

Some auctions are going to start with a minimum bid, and the people who have an interest in the auction (facility owner) might not want to part with the items for less than a certain amount (maybe to recoup some lost rent from the former tenant).

If there is NOT a minimum bid at the auction, which is the case almost all of the time, this is how I handle the bidding process:

The first rule of bidding is, DO NOT SPEAK UP the first time the auctioneer opens up the bidding. **REMEMBER:** The auctioneer is on commission! The auctioneer will try to start as high as possible, to get the highest price he can, which is not necessarily the best for you.

So wait until after the auctioneer drops the price down a bit, and you have a few options. First, you can wait until another bidder opens up the bidding and then start your own bidding. An example of this situation might be: The auctioneer opens up bidding on a locker at $100, and if nobody says anything, it will drop down to $50. Be patient; the opening bid will lower to $25 if people stay quiet.

A second option is to speak up right after the auctioneer has dropped the price the first time. In the above example, you would want to speak up at $50. Hopefully, it is high enough to scare anyone else away.

The final option on bidding (I find this one has the best results!) is to open up with a super-LOW bid BEFORE the auctioneer starts the bidding. For example, when you see the majority of the crowd has viewed the locker, you might want to say to the auctioneer, "I'll give you $5." Keep in mind that you will get a reaction from the auctioneer, but at least your offer is in and the bidding has started low. This option seems to result in the least number of people bidding against you, and you are not stepping on many people's toes.

While we are on this subject: In my opinion, the bidding process from auction to auction becomes very political. People DO remember who wins lockers and how many they have won. So, I will give you a word of caution – if someone asks, "How did you do on that last locker you won?" ALWAYS answer, "I barely broke even." Most likely, the person who lost the locker to you will be the one asking.

Now you know how to open a bid up, let's win a locker…and make some money!

Never start bidding without an exit plan. As soon as you start bidding, have a number in your head: the highest number you are willing to go up to. You will come up with it when you have seen the contents of the locker, and thus know what you can sell to recoup your costs.

Never stray very far from the number you have come up with. Two things tend to happen if you do:

1. You stretch to break even on the locker.

2. If the locker turns out to be a flop, you just cleaned out a unit for the storage facility for free.

What if the owner of the locker shows up?

If the owner of a locker shows up at an auction…get EXCITED, because this happens for one of two reasons. The first reason might be because they have sentimental things like family photos and other mementos in the locker. The second reason might be that there is something valuable in the locker.

If you win the locker, there are a few ways to handle this situation:

1. Sell the locker back to the owner; just add money to what you paid. For example, if you paid $200 for the locker, add $300. You have instantly made $300 and you did not even have to touch anything. You will still want to make sure the locker gets unloaded, because you are responsible for it.

2. If you see that you can make more money by the normal streams of distribution, such as eBay, Amazon, or a sale, then pass on the owner's offer to buy it back. A word of caution here: If you do so, you will want to get that locker unloaded as quickly as possible. I do not care how secure you think the storage facility is; old owners break in and steal their stuff back all the time.

3. Sell back a portion of the locker to the owner.

Some helpful tips to keep in mind:

1. If the stuff in the locker looks like junk, if there are boxes open and trash on the ground, that usually means it has already been gone through and the good stuff has already been taken.

2. Do NOT split the lockers with any other auction attendees! It is very difficult to split the individual items, especially before looking in the locker at the auction. You very well may end up on the short end of the stick, especially if you are new at this.

3. Since this is a business, make sure you are not giving too many items to your friends and family. Most will understand that you need to make a living, and also have some money on hand for the next auction.

4. I cannot stress this too many times… **do not tell other auction attendees everything you got in a locker!** Let other people tell you what they got, and find out how they sold it. Most are more

than happy to talk about it. The benefit is twofold: First, you will learn where you can sell some things. Second, you are not showing too much of your hand by sharing all the wonderful treasures you have found. If you are itching to show off your treasures, take pictures of them and submit them to our Web site instead.

5. Before the auctions, make light conversation with people. At each auction, talk to someone different and get to know them. This will make you personable to other attendees, and hopefully they will think twice about bidding against you, since you are such a nice guy or girl.

6. ANY new attendees raise eyebrows at the auction; you just have to act like you belong there. Many of the fellow auction-goers have attended for many years and know who is a regular.

7. My best advice is to attend at least two auctions (no more than five), before bidding. You should win at least one really nice locker within ten bids.

8. If you want a locker, open up the bidding! You might get one or two people bidding against you, but just try it and see what happens!

9. Also, take a mental note of who is bidding and how high they go on lockers. This information might help you later.

Chapter 3

"CRAP! I Won – NOW What????"

You might feel a bit faint at first after winning your first auction, but just put your lock on the locker and get ready for a great time! I have put together a few steps that will help you.

Breathe! Your mind will be racing with all sorts of questions, starting with "How am I going to do this?!" Here is where reading this book will help you tremendously.

First, confirm how long you have to clear out the locker, because it will play a big role in how quickly you get everything done. Depending on the storage place, the time period ranges from twenty-four hours up to whatever you can negotiate. On larger units, usually the manager will give you one to two weeks to empty. You do not want to make a career out of pulling stuff out, but you do not want to run short on time either.

If the unit is large or you are limited on time to unload, you can actually rent the locker yourself if the storage facility is running a special.

If you have negotiated a week or more, good for you! You could fit your unloading into a Saturday or Sunday without messing with the week's auction schedule or your daytime job.

However, if you only have a day or two, this is where the challenge comes in. For starters, you need to decide where you are going to go through this stuff. If you have a holding area, then you'll just pack up your items and drop them off there. You will then be able to go through everything at your leisure.

Remember, you get out of this what you put in. So if you're willing to give up an evening of reruns on television, you might find treasures in your boxes!

If you are tight on space, going through everything gets a bit tricky, but it can still be done. You will just have to separate the stuff on site. The best piece of advice I can give you is to get a gate code, so you have longer access to the locker. Try to get it done fairly quickly, because now you will be going through a locker, instead of attending auctions. Nonetheless, if there is a really good locker that you have heard of, try to make it to the auction.

When you are sorting, here are a few things to remember. Put some good music on and keep it moving. I usually set up five piles.

1. Donation Pile (Goodwill, Salvation Army)
2. Dump Pile

3. Personal Effects Pile
4. eBay and Amazon Pile
5. Garage Sale Pile

PILE #1: Donation Pile – Some donation places will pick up, or you can drop off. You should call and find out ahead of time what they do not take. This is a great idea for older clothes and other non-sellable items. Make sure you get a receipt for tax deduction purposes.

PILE #2: Dump Pile – If you have an excess of empty boxes, use them to package up the trash. You will want to find an inexpensive way to dump, because your dump fees can quickly add up. Check your local dump and see what their prices for city residents are, or make friends with the people doing the weighing at the dump.

If you have large items, you might want to call the city and see if they will pick up for a fee. Also, check to see if there are citywide pickups during the year, and if so, when they are.

Also, you can ask the storage facility if you can use their on-site dumpster.

Finally, you might want to look into craigslist.org for getting rid of big items that do not sell fast.

PILE #3: Personal Effects Pile - You will want to return ALL of the former owner's personal papers and photographs. This is not required, but it is always appreciated.

PILE #4: eBay/Amazon Pile - This pile is of items that you will be able to sell on eBay or Amazon. When you log onto the eBay Web site, it can seem a bit intimidating. There are a zillion books you can buy on how to sell on eBay, but personally, I didn't buy a book and just jumped in, figuring it out as I went.

One thing I do when I have an item I would like to sell on eBay is to look it up on the eBay Web site. I do this for two reasons: first, to see if the item I have is worth selling, and second, to see how well other people are selling the item. eBay makes listing pretty self-explanatory, so I would advise against hiring an eBay sales assistant or spending lots of money on going to eBay's training on how to list products.

You should get five or ten items together and take pictures, then set up the listing of each one. Thus, at the end of your auctions, you have a group of items that you can invoice and package up, all at the same time.

I have observed that more people shop on eBay during the weekends and evenings, so set your auctions up accordingly.

Helpful Hints:

1. Set up auctions on a seven-day time period, to make sure you have a weekend in there.

2. End auctions in the early evening, say, from 5 PM – 7 PM.

3. Your ideal ending time would be Sunday, around 5 PM.

If, after listing a few eBay auctions, you decide it is not for you, you can use a company that lists auctions for you. Locally, we have a place called Auction Drop. They take a certain percentage of the profit to pay for the listing, and you get the rest.

The second option is hiring a sales assistant through eBay. They will charge for their services, though, and this adds up.

Now for the Amazon section of your pile: books, CDs, DVDs, videotapes, and computer games.

If you get a locker that has boxes and boxes of books, you may be able to open up your own Amazon shop. If you do, you will want to see if it makes financial sense to be an Amazon Pro Merchant, which means you pay one flat rate and pay a lower commission per book. If you decide that you do not have enough books for Pro

Merchant status, Amazon's commission per book will be higher. If you already have books listed and decide to change over to Pro Merchant status, not to worry! Each non-Pro Merchant listing expires in sixty days, at which time you can put a SKU number on the book for inventory purposes.

When listing your books on Amazon, you will want to start a SKU system to help you pull the books when you sell them. I use banker boxes and put ten to fifteen books in each, then label the box with something like SKU #Box 2.

Again, there are a zillion books about selling on Amazon, but it is up to you to decide if you really need one. Listing on Amazon, like listing on eBay, is pretty self-explanatory. I advise that you just go to the homepage, click on Sell Your Stuff, and follow the directions.

Pile #5: Garage Sale Pile – This pile will be furniture, items that you did not sell via the Internet, and all other miscellaneous sellable items.

I have a truck where I store all my sellable items, and follow this simple rule: When the truck is full, hold a garage sale.

Preparation for a sale

You will want to advertise in local papers, put up neighborhood signs, and post listings on *craigslist.org*.

Make sure you start advertising a few days before the sale is to be held, so people can plan to attend.

Benefits to having a garage sale

1. You do not have to get up extra early and wait in line at the Flea Market.

2. You can set up the day before; just securely tarp the tables overnight.

3. You get to know your neighbors.

4. Some customers will give you contact information, because they collect a certain item and are always curious to see what you find in the lockers.

Setting up your sale

You will want to organize your sale with different sections, and perhaps include a flat-rate table. For example, I usually have a $1-per-item table, and a box of children's toys which is priced twenty-five cents each or six for a dollar.

When figuring out pricing, I have a rule of thumb: Make the price about 30 percent of what you would pay for it in a store.

If you don't live on a busy corner or just don't get enough traffic to have a garage sale, you may want to sell your items at a flea market. Look for listings at your local high schools and colleges, and when you attend, make sure you bring bags and some folding tables.

Other tips for any kind of sale:

1. Do not price everything; this will open the lines of communication between you and the customer.

2. Be flexible on price; remember, you want to keep your items moving!

3. Have discounts; tell your customers that the more they buy, the more they save!

4. After 1 PM, make everything half-off!

5. Sometimes you will find collectors coming up and giving you their contact information; encourage this!

Chapter 4

What a Typical Week Should Look Like

I wanted to show you what a week SHOULD look like in a perfect world, just so you have something to aspire to. If you find that it does not fit your schedule, it is completely customizable, but please remember that things will not always go as planned.

You are going to have some weeks that are full of junk lockers, cancellations, and scheduling conflicts. Do not lose heart; a superb locker is right around the corner!

What you need to be doing in any given week…

1. Attend auctions

2. Once a locker is won, empty it

3. Go through the contents of locker

4. List on eBay and/or Amazon

5. Have a sale

You will need a truck or van, depending on the size of the locker. Here are some of your options:

1. Buy a truck/van

2. Rent a truck/van

3. Rent a trailer

You are going to need a place to sort. If there is not one on site, you will need to take your stuff to a warehouse, some other storage facility or a garage. You can also use your own backyard, but you need to keep a watch on the weather. Some things can get ruined in the sun, like furniture, and almost anything can get ruined in the rain.

When unloading a locker, the easiest method is to unload the items and take them to a sorting area yourself. If it is a larger locker, you might consider hiring another person to help, because it gives you someone to talk to, and the unloading goes twice as fast. You may want to consider hiring a high school or college student, or a worker from one of the local home improvement stores.

A Typical Week:

Monday	Attend auctions
Tuesday	Attend auctions Unload items from auctions won on Monday
Wednesday	Attend auctions Unload items from auctions won on Tuesday Go through items
Thursday	Attend auctions Unload items from auctions won on Wednesday
Friday	Finish going through items Prepare for flea market or garage sale Make a dump run
Saturday	Hold a garage sale or go to a flea market

Try to keep lockers in the pipeline, so you will always have inventory.

Chapter 5

Some Valuable Tips

If you treat this business like a business, there is some serious cash to be made. I have made a list of things to keep in mind:

1. Reinvest back into your business.

    a. Keep cash on you for the auctions, and buy the equipment you will need.

2. Have a full knowledge of a locker's value—know what to sell and what to toss.

3. Have the patience to wait for and buy better-quality lockers.

4. Have a steady a flow of lockers.

Additional tip…

If you have gone to auctions all week long and have no lockers to show for it, for various reasons like the locker prices went too high, there was no way you were going to make a profit, or you saw nothing but junk, DO NOT get discouraged…it happens to everyone. The very next week, you may show up to an auction where there was no one else, and get a fabulous locker for a buck!

Another tip…

You have heard the saying that loose lips sink ships, and that totally applies here. If you hear of any auctions not on the list, or if you hear any additional information about a locker, DO NOT say a word to anybody. Just like in poker, keep your hand close to you.

A third tip…

When you are waiting for an auction to start, watch what you say to people. It is very political, and people can get angry or jealous very easily. You definitely do not want to brag about a locker that you did particularly well with. Once the auction starts, people do not forget stuff like that, and will sometimes run you up on a locker just to be spiteful.

I hope you will find all the tips I have given you helpful. Now the trick to getting started with auctions is for you to just step out and do it! You will learn something new with every auction and every locker.

I am currently working on a Web site. There is a link at the site to e-mail me and let me know about all the wonderful treasures you find; make sure you send pictures, and I will add them to the Web site!

www.selfstorageauctioncash.com

Epilogue

I whole heartedly send congratulations to you for finishing this book!

I can see that you are an absolute go-getter, just by getting this far.

Now let's keep your momentum going…

Check out this book's full service website at http://www.selfstorageauctioncash.com! Thoughtfully packaged resources to get you up and running fast along with value-added packages are available 24 hours a day. These carefully crafted packages include an autographed copy of the book, an online homestudy course that can be completed at any hour of the day, and email access to me to answer any questions you may have.

Why did I bother creating this website for you? I want to be able to answer your questions as you get your self storage auction business up and running. When I started out with this business, I had no one to ask. I had no one to compare notes with. And - I had no one to mentor me.

Stop by and say hello! I'm here to help you so that you can build your business fast.

This business is super easy—if you know what to do. Anyone can go to the auctions, bid and win a locker. You are head and shoulders above your fellow bidders because you have cracked the code for winning in your self storage auction business. With this book, you have all the secrets over "everyone". You know how to win a locker and make it into a profitable, productive business. If you use the information that is available to you within these pages and the website, you WILL make boxes of cash with self-storage auctions.

Lots of Lucrative Lockers!
Barbara